Birthday Boy

by Christopher Slade Newbound

A Samuel French Acting Edition

SAMUELFRENCH.COM

Copyright © 2013 by Christopher Slade Newbound
ALL RIGHTS RESERVED

CAUTION: Professionals and amateurs are hereby warned that *BIRTHDAY BOY* is subject to a licensing fee. It is fully protected under the copyright laws of the United States of America, the British Commonwealth, including Canada, and all other countries of the Copyright Union. All rights, including professional, amateur, motion picture, recitation, lecturing, public reading, radio broadcasting, television and the rights of translation into foreign languages are strictly reserved. In its present form the play is dedicated to the reading public only.

The amateur and professional live stage performance rights to *BIRTHDAY BOY* are controlled exclusively by Samuel French, Inc., and licensing arrangements and performance licenses must be secured well in advance of presentation. PLEASE NOTE that amateur licensing fees are set upon application in accordance with your producing circumstances. When applying for a licensing quotation and a performance license please give us the number of performances intended, dates of production, your seating capacity and admission fee. Licensing fees are payable one week before the opening performance of the play to Samuel French, Inc., at 45 W. 25th Street, New York, NY 10010.

Licensing fee of the required amount must be paid whether the play is presented for charity or gain and whether or not admission is charged.

Professional/Stock licensing fees quoted upon application to Samuel French, Inc.

For all other rights than those stipulated above, apply to: Charles Van Nostrand, PO Box 117, Woodbourne, NY 12788.

Particular emphasis is laid on the question of amateur or professional readings, permission and terms for which must be secured in writing from Samuel French, Inc.

Copying from this book in whole or in part is strictly forbidden by law, and the right of performance is not transferable.

Whenever the play is produced the following notice must appear on all programs, printing and advertising for the play: "Produced by special arrangement with Samuel French, Inc."

Due authorship credit must be given on all programs, printing and advertising for the play.

ISBN 978-0-573-70109-2   Printed in U.S.A.   #20533

No one shall commit or authorize any act or omission by which the copyright of, or the right to copyright, this play may be impaired.

No one shall make any changes in this play for the purpose of production.

Publication of this play does not imply availability for performance. Both amateurs and professionals considering a production are strongly advised in their own interests to apply to Samuel French, Inc., for written permission before starting rehearsals, advertising, or booking a theatre.

No part of this book may be reproduced, stored in a retrieval system, or transmitted in any form, by any means, now known or yet to be invented, including mechanical, electronic, photocopying, recording, videotaping, or otherwise, without the prior written permission of the publisher.

MUSIC USE NOTE

Licensees are solely responsible for obtaining formal written permission from copyright owners to use copyrighted music in the performance of this play and are strongly cautioned to do so. If no such permission is obtained by the licensee, then the licensee must use only original music that the licensee owns and controls. Licensees are solely responsible and liable for all music clearances and shall indemnify the copyright owners of the play and their licensing agent, Samuel French, Inc., against any costs, expenses, losses and liabilities arising from the use of music by licensees.

IMPORTANT BILLING AND CREDIT REQUIREMENTS

All producers of *BIRTHDAY BOY* must give credit to the Author of the Play in all programs distributed in connection with performances of the Play, and in all instances in which the title of the Play appears for the purposes of advertising, publicizing or otherwise exploiting the Play and/or a production. The name of the Author *must* appear on a separate line on which no other name appears, immediately following the title and *must* appear in size of type not less than fifty percent of the size of the title type.

BIRTHDAY BOY received its professional world premiere at Berkshire Theatre Festival, Unicorn Theatre (Kate Maguire, Artistic Director) in Stockbridge, MA, in August, 2011. The performance was directed by Wes Grantom, with sets by Kenneth Grady Barker, costumes by Charles Schoonmaker, lighting by Derek Wright, and sound by Phil Pickens. The Production Stage Manager was Kyle S. Urquhart. The cast was as follows:

JULIAN . . . . Nick Dillenburg
MELORA . . . . Tara Franklin
MATT . . . . James Ludwig
ARIANNE . . . . Keira Naughton

CHARACTERS

MATT – About to turn forty.
MELORA – About to turn thirty, a colleague of Matt's.
ARIANNE – Matt's Wife
JULIAN – Student of Arianne's, in his twenties.

SETTING

The lunchroom where Matt and Melora work.
A bar of a Mexican restaurant: Mi Casa Su Casa.
Bedroom of Matt and Arianne's house.
A hospital room.

TIME

The present.

AUTHOR'S NOTES

The play is in two acts, and can be performed with or without an intermission.

ACT ONE
Scene One

(Setting: The lunchroom inside the offices of a fairly successful start-up webzine communications company in a small Western city.)

(At rise: **MATT** *is alone doing pushups and/or sit-ups on the floor of the lunchroom wearing headphones. He is dressed in winter running clothes, running tights, long-sleeve shirt with hat and gloves. He is an athletic, youthful, almost forty.* **MELORA,** *an attractive woman about to turn thirty and a new colleague of* **MATT**'s, *enters without* **MATT** *noticing her. She is dressed in casual, but nice work clothes. She starts to get food from the fridge, puts food on plate, microwaves, and finally sits down with her lunch throughout. After* **MATT** *finally notices her, a bit embarrassed, he moves to table to resume eating his lunch.)*

MELORA. Hi.

MATT. *(loud)* Hey. I didn't see you come in.

(awkward pause as **MELORA** *continues to prepare her lunch)*

MELORA. *(finally)* So, you went running?

MATT. I did. And then I was doing some...

MELORA. *(She gives him a look.)* Well don't stop on my account.

MATT. I was more or less done.

MELORA. So how far did you go?

MATT. Three, maybe four?

*(***MELORA*** nods, not terribly impressed and then turns back to the microwave. It dings. Throughout the*

*following, she'll get her food ready, and settle at the table across from **MATT**.)*

MATT. *(cont.)* So how you liking the new job?

MELORA. I'm liking it. But not quite so new, anymore.

MATT. No? How long's it been then?

MELORA. Three months.

MATT. Really? It seems like it's been…less. Less than three months somehow.

MELORA. Well, not to me…

MATT. …Like you started just last month, or something?

MELORA. November 12th.

MATT. Sorry?

MELORA. My start date was November 12th.

MATT. Ah. Well. Time sure plods along even when you're not having fun, I guess is the moral to that story.

MELORA. *(amused)* So you don't like it around here?

MATT. Oh. No. It's fine. You know for a job and all. But I've been here four years, so…

MELORA. Wow. I don't think I've been in any job for four years.

MATT. Have you even been out of college four years?

*(**MELORA** smiles.)*

(pause)

*(**MATT** fingers a magazine next to his food.)*

MELORA. Don't let me interrupt…from your…I mean. Feel free to…

MATT. Oh, no. Just a prop. You know should someone who I don't want to talk to come around.

MELORA. Ah. Glad I rate. *(after another long pause)* It's kind of weird, you know, how they have just the one lunch table.

MATT. It's very Shaker like. Or is that Mormon? I can never keep those two straight. Supposed to create a sense of community. Informal, collegial, an opportunity for peers to mix and exchange information in a casual, collegial way.

(pause)

MELORA. *(finally)* So different from my last job.

MATT. Which was…?

MELORA. I worked for this national tea company, assistant to head of marketing there, and it was just a lot more formal, I guess. A lot more corporate. You know. Dress code. Suits. Ties. Forty people on a floor. Everyone had assistants and it was very hierarchical, I guess you could say. No one spoke to one another unless they absolutely had to. Not even by phone. If you needed to communicate with anyone, you did so by e-mail, or…

MATT. *(trying to help out)* Or…?

MELORA. *(a bit embarrassed)* Or…I don't know. I have no idea what I was going to say.

MATT. Sign language, perhaps? By smoke signal?…So why'd you leave? Because of all the smoke detectors going off all the time?

MELORA. Ron. My husband Ron, he got transferred.

MATT. Ah. So what's he do?

*(***MELORA** *hesitates, shrugs.)*

Tough question?

MELORA. A computer programmer, I guess? Something in software?

(awkward pause)

MATT. So this must be a bit of a change? You must have been in shock after the first colleague meeting.

MELORA. A little more touchy-feely than I'm used to.

MATT. Which part? The sitting cross-legged on the floor, allowing dogs to the meeting so they can slobber all over everyone, or just going around the room and everyone "sharing" what they all did with their weekends before getting down to business? A bit of pressure, don't you think? I mean that's the way I remember feeling at first. I better have a damn good weekend, or else.

(after **MELORA** *doesn't respond)*

MATT. *(cont.)* Not that I didn't have damn good weekends. I mean, occasionally I had some pretty darn good ones

(another long pause, while they eat in silence)

MELORA. So how long have you been running for?

MATT. Oh forever. I guess off and on since, well, I was probably your age.

MELORA. I don't think I'm quite as young as you seem to think I am.

MATT. I'm sorry. It's just that when you get to a certain age, everyone starts looking really young.

MELORA. And what age is that?

MATT. I've got a birthday coming up. A big one...I'm turning forty in about a month.

MELORA. Ah.

*(**MATT** waits expectantly.)*

MATT. *(finally)* So now is when you're supposed to say, somewhat shocked if you would be so kind, "Gee Matt. You've got to be kidding. You don't look forty. Not even close. How can you be forty?"

MELORA. Well, you don't look forty. But I don't think forty's so old.

MATT. ...said the girl who looks like she just got out of college. *(after a beat)* The new thirty-five?

*(**MELORA** waits, not understanding.)*

You know...the thing about forty being the new thirty-five?

*(**MELORA** nods.)*

(awkward pause)

MELORA. *(finally)* We should run together sometime.

MATT. Yeah?

MELORA. We *shouldn't* run together sometime?

MATT. No. I mean. Sure. I mean we should. We *should* run together sometime. Definitely.

(MATT *watches* MELORA *already finishing up her lunch, starting to get up to wash her dish in the sink, getting ready to leave.*)

When?

MELORA. What?

MATT. When would we, do this? When would we run together sometime? Although we could be incompatible, you know. *(quickly adding)* Fitness wise, I mean.

MELORA. You don't think I can keep up? I ran a marathon last fall, I'll have you know.

MATT. And I'll have you know that I *did not* run a marathon last fall...You ran a marathon? Really? That's impressive. Did you finish?

(She smiles. Of course she finished.)

But did you enjoy it? Or did you pee, or bleed, or throw up all over yourself?

MELORA. Actually, it was one of the best experiences of my life.

MATT. Like labor? Worth it in the end?

MELORA. How 'bout I e-mail you. About running together sometime.

MATT. Sure. Or you could send up a smoke signal. And in the meantime, I'll try and quickly get in shape, and/or, you know, get a lot younger somehow. There must be some performance-enhancing herbs hidden around here somewhere.

(She checks him out, smiles.)

MELORA. I'm sure you'll be able to keep up.

(MELORA *exits.* MATT *goes back to eating alone: picks up his magazine, can't concentrate. He resumes doing some sit ups, starts slowly and then is doing them very fast as we...Fade out.*)

(*The Police's* Every Move You Make *plays loudly in between scene changes. "I'll be watching you."*)[*]

---

[*]See Music Use Note on page 3.

Scene Two

(Setting: Same lunchroom. A few weeks later.)

*(At rise: **MATT** and **MELORA** are sitting eating their lunch only this time they're both dressed in running clothes, post run, in the middle of talking.)*

MATT. What? I feel like you're upset with me or something. Like I let you down. I just didn't feel like I had time to go another *three* miles?

MELORA. The time or the inclination?

MATT. Time…or inclination, given that I didn't have the time. You could have kept running, you know. I wasn't lost or incoherent or anything. I probably could have found my way back to the office. How far do you usually run, anyway?

*(after **MELORA** stays quiet)*

Come on. How far do you usually go? I can take it. Six?…Eight?…*Fifteen?*

MELORA. It varies. And I really didn't want to get my heart rate up above 150 anyway, so it was good. It was good for me to have a recovery day.

MATT. So that was slow for you? That was you taking it easy on me out there. That was you *recovering?*

*(**MATT** gives her a look, not letting her off the hook.)*

MELORA. So I've been running a little more than you.

MATT. And now you'll never run with me again, *he said, hopefully…*

(a beat)

MELORA. Hey, did you get my e-mail?

MATT. About…?

MELORA. Friday.

*(**MATT** is still confused.)*

Drinks? Mi Casa, Su Casa?

MATT. Oh, yeah. I think it'll work. So what's the occasion again?

MELORA. "What's the occasion?" Only your fortieth and my thirtieth.

MATT. I still can't get my head around that number. I mean I can remember my parents turning forty. Like not that long ago. And they're old now. I mean they're seriously old. You should run with *them* sometime. Every day's a recovery day for them.

MELORA. Forty's not old.

MATT. …"Said the thirty-year-old."

MELORA. Twenty-nine until next Tuesday. Don't rush me.

MATT. I can't believe our birthday's are so close together.

MELORA. Must be why we're so compatible. *(after an awkward pause, trying to be nonchalant)* So is Andrea going to be able to make it?

MATT. Andrea?

MELORA. Shit. For a marketing person, I'm really bad with names. *(after she waits)* So you're not going to tell me what your wife's name is?

MATT. Arianne.

MELORA. Arianne. Well that's very pretty. Is she pretty? You know, pretty like her name?

MATT. She's ah…yeah.

MELORA. She's ah…yeah?

MATT. She's pretty.

MELORA. How pretty?

MATT. How pretty? I don't know. Like on the nationally recognized pretty meter, you mean? She's pretty. Pretty, pretty I guess.

MELORA. Well, I'd love to finally meet her. Meet your pretty, pretty wife.

MATT. Well, we've got a sitter coming on Saturday, my actual birthday. So two nights in a row could be pushing it with the kids.

MELORA. *(as she gets up and starts to stretch with her back to him, working out a calf cramp or something)* And kids, too? Well, at least you've been keeping busy for an old man. Kids. Wow. How old are your kids?

MATT. Cal's ten and Melissa's…

(**MATT** *becomes distracted by discreetly checking out* **MELORA**'s *behind as she bends over in a stretch.*)

MELORA. What are you doing?

MATT. *(feeling caught)* What?

MELORA. *(as she turns back to him)* For your actual birthday. What are you doing for the actual day?

MATT. Oh. Some place called the Fawn Brook Inn. I think it's like some six-course dinner. You get to eat a lot of small animals from what I gather. Although I don't think you actually have to kill them yourself. My understanding is that they do that for you. Road kill perhaps? I'll gain like five pounds in one night. But, you know big fireplace. Rustic. Way up in the mountains somewhere. I just hope it doesn't snow.

MELORA. You going with a ton of friends?

MATT. Friends? No. I don't really have those.

MELORA. What, are you like not a nice person or something?

MATT. I have friends. I just don't really like them as much as I used to. I think I need to, oh I don't know, trade them in. Get a fresh batch. Go back to the friend factory or something.

MELORA. Friend factory?

MATT. Probably not possible, right? Maybe it's just a phase I'm going through. Anyway, I wanted it to be just the two of us…Arianne and I.

MELORA. Sounds nice. Sounds romantic.

MATT. So what about you? What about you and Ron? For your birthday.

MELORA. I think we're having a few friends over. We have some. Friends. Even a few that we still sort of like. But my real birthday present is our trip. We just can't get away until March.

MATT. Where you going?

MELORA. Mexico. Scuba diving in Cancun.

MATT. Wow. You run marathons *and* scuba dive?

MELORA. Ron's more into than I am.

MATT. That doesn't make you a little nervous? Being so far underwater like that?

MELORA. Oh sure. A little. But you know what they say? "Life shrinks or expands in proportion to one's courage."

MATT. Anais Nin.

MELORA. *(impressed)* Yes.

(They take a moment.)

Well I hope she can make it on Friday. Arianne, I mean. I'd love to finally meet her.

MATT *(deadpan)* Adrian.

MELORA. Adrian? Shut up.

(MATT laughs.)

Nice. Now I know why you don't have any friends. Why you need to revisit the "friend factory."

MATT. But that doesn't mean there won't be a quiz later on because this is obviously still giving you some trouble.

MELORA. *(finally)* So, any thoughts on the other thing?

(MATT has no idea what she's talking about.)

Do you even read my e-mails?

MATT. Remember the good old days when people actually talked to one another?

MELORA. Getting my belly button pierced for my thirtieth?

MATT. Sorry, was I supposed to get back to you on that?

MELORA. Only if you felt strongly one way or the other.

MATT. Sorry, but what exactly is the purpose of them anyway? Pierced belly buttons.

MELORA. Purpose? You don't like them then?

MATT. No. I mean I don't know. I guess I don't really have a strong "for" or "against" position. Which is probably why I never bothered to e-mail you back about it.

MELORA. Arianne doesn't have one I take it.

MATT. *(amused)* No. Arianne does not. Arianne doesn't like anyone going near her navel as a matter of fact. Not even me.

MELORA. *(amused)* Why?

MATT. No one really knows for sure. Just a very sensitive spot for her, for some reason. Probably some deep-seated trauma relating to her umbilical cord at birth that not even she's aware of.

(The two eat in silence for a while.)

MELORA. *(finally; offhand, shy)* Some people think they're sort of sexy, I guess.

(a beat)

Hey I have sort of a favor to ask. My car's getting serviced on Friday. And so, any chance you might give me a ride on Friday? I mean if it's not too much of a hassle.

MATT. Oh. No. No hassle.

MELORA. It's the side mirror. You can't adjust it from the inside.

MATT. Ah.

MELORA. And the passenger seat heating is totally messed up. It heats up way too much.

MATT. Those things have always made me a little nervous for some reason.

MELORA. What things?

MATT. Those heated-seat things. Every time I'm sitting in one of them and it heats up…I think I've just soiled myself.

MELORA. Really.

MATT. Not that I think I've *actually* soiled myself. Just that it feels like I *might* have…soiled myself. So…I take it you'll be needing a ride *home* as well?

MELORA. No. I mean, yes, well, maybe. But if you want to take off before me, or vice versa, I'm sure I can get someone else to give me a ride home. I mean won't you have some sort of curfew?

MATT. Curfew? No. I mean who would begrudge me my one night out with all my best friends from work to help celebrate the big "four oh."

MELORA. *(checking her watch)* Oh, shit.

(**MATT** *just waits.*)

Marketing meeting at two. Don't tell me. You can't make this one either.

MATT. I always felt that "attendance optional" sort of meant, well, you know, "attendance optional".

(**MELORA** *just gives him a look.*)

I'm shy in groups.

MELORA. I'll bet. So Friday?

MATT. Friday?

MELORA. Mi Casa Su Casa?

(**MATT** *nods. She smiles, exits.*)

MATT. *(to himself)* 'Soiled myself?'

(*Lights fade as Billy Joel's* For the Longest Time *plays throughout.*)*

---

*See Music Use Note on page 3.

Scene Three

*(Setting: The Friday before **MATT**'s fortieth birthday. A snowy winter evening in February just after work, at Mi Casa, Su Casa, a Mexican restaurant. And the bedroom of the home of **MATT** and **ARIANNE**.)*

*(At rise: **MELORA** is sitting at the end of the table on one side of the stage, but in darkness. Presumably there are a lot of other colleagues sitting at the other side of the table, offstage. She is nursing a frozen margarita, eating chips and salsa. **MATT** is dressed in typical office work clothes, casual but maybe with a tie. **MELORA** is the same, although she has made more of an attempt to dress for "going out." There is music playing from some jukebox. The place will occasionally get so noisy that **MATT** and **MELORA** will have to sometimes lean in and speak loudly in order to be heard. When the lights come up on **MATT**, he is on the other side of the stage, using his cell phone. He has a finger in the ear that's not pressed to the phone. As the phone rings and rings, **ARIANNE** finally enters their bedroom in the middle of the stage to answer the ringing phone. She seems a bit giddy herself as she rushes in. Perhaps even laughing at something one of her children has just said. She is also slightly dressed up and is putting an earring on as she talks.)*

ARIANNE. Hello you.

MATT. Took you long enough to answer.

ARIANNE. We're all set by the way.

MATT. Set? You mean for life?

ARIANNE. Four non-refundable round-trip tickets to Burlington, get in on the nineteenth of April and get home the twenty-sixth.

MATT. Vermont. So that's good news. About Vermont I mean. No wonder you sound like you're in such a good mood.

ARIANNE. Do I sound in a good mood?

MATT. Kind of. But then you always do when I'm not around. Why is that, I wonder?

ARIANNE. That's a lie. Where are you?

MATT. Out. You know, with all my good friends from work.

ARIANNE. You like some of them.

MATT. How are the kids?

ARIANNE. Oh Matt. That's so sweet that you remembered we have children.

MATT. "Go Matt. Have fun. It's your birthday." So how are they? Missing me terribly of course.

ARIANNE. Where are you again?

MATT. Mi Casa, Su Casa.

ARIANNE. Are you going to have dinner there?

MATT. We may get around to eating eventually. You may have forgotten this, I know I did, but that's what people without children like to do on Friday nights. They drink and *then* if there's time, they sometimes get around to eating more solid food.

(A doorbell can be heard ringing. **ARIANNE***, hearing it turns around, distracted.)*

ARIANNE. *(calling to the kids, presumably)* CAN SOMEBODY GET THAT?

MATT. Arianne?

ARIANNE. Sorry.

MATT. Is someone there?

ARIANNE. Ah…Pizza guy. So when will you be home again?

MATT. I don't know…around nine, nine-thirty?

ARIANNE. Don't forget that you promised Melissa that you'd be home at nine to listen to her piano piece. Her recital's this Monday, you know.

MATT. You'll still be up?

ARIANNE. Doubtful. But I'll worry if you're not home.

MATT. You worry in your sleep?

ARIANNE. I'll worry when I'm dead.

MATT. Nice.

ARIANNE. Are you consuming lots and lots of alcohol?

MATT. Maybe just lots. Why? Do I sound drunk?

ARIANNE. No more goofy than usual.

MATT. Remember when we used to drink together?

ARIANNE. We still drink together.

MATT. I mean really drink.

ARIANNE. That was just so we could get naked in front of each other at first and not feel completely mortified. I mean I don't recall us being alcoholics or anything.

(a beat)

Hey, I'm sorry I've been so intense about the whole, you know, Vermont thing. I'll try and lighten up.

MATT. Now that we've got tickets to go there in April. I think we're like the only people in America who are dying to go to Vermont for mud season.

ARIANNE. So I'll see you later?

MATT. Yeah.

ARIANNE. Nine. Right?

MATT. Jesus, Arianne. How many times you going to say it?

ARIANNE. I love you.

MATT. What? Okay. I mean, I love you too.

*(**ARIANNE** hangs up abruptly and then **MATT** hangs up slowly. Lights fade on **MATT**. **ARIANNE** turns around in her bedroom to find **JULIAN MOODY** standing in the doorway watching her, holding a skateboard. She is startled to find him there. He is a graduate student in his mid-twenties, attractive in a rugged, outdoorsy way.)*

JULIAN. Hello.

ARIANNE. You're not the Pizza guy.

JULIAN. Now that would be quite a coincidence wouldn't it? Me delivering a Pizza to your house.

ARIANNE. What are you doing here?

JULIAN. If I'm not the Pizza guy? I was…in the neighborhood?

ARIANNE. How did you get in?

JULIAN. Well your kids seemed to be under the impression that I am the Pizza guy.

ARIANNE. But you're not.

JULIAN. Haven't we already covered this? Look I didn't say I was the Pizza guy, I just didn't really deny it either. Cute kids by the way. They yours?

ARIANNE. Who else would they belong to?

JULIAN. The neighbors? I've never really thought of you as a Mom before. I'm seeing you in a whole new light here. It's not necessarily bad. Just…different.

ARIANNE *(only now noticing)* What did you do to your hair?

JULIAN. I cut it. What? You don't like it?

ARIANNE. Short, is all.

JULIAN. You don't like it.

ARIANNE. No. I do. It looks good. I mean it looks *fine*.

JULIAN. So was that your husband? Who you were talking with on the phone? So he's ah…

ARIANNE. Out.

JULIAN. Ah. Out. How convenient. For us, I mean.

ARIANNE. You really can't be here, you know. I'm sorry, but you're going to have to leave now.

JULIAN. But I just got here.

ARIANNE. You came all this way on your skateboard?

JULIAN. It's not that far. Six miles. Well, six point four miles to be exact.

ARIANNE. *(slightly thrown)* Well, that's the risk you take when you just drop in on people. Sorry Julian, but this just isn't a very convenient time.

JULIAN. You really want me to leave?

ARIANNE. I thought after our little talk the other day, we'd kind of gotten things straightened out. That there weren't going to be any more, you know, misunderstandings. Any confusion here. No more you suddenly appearing.

JULIAN. I miss you. I miss seeing you. I miss our conferences. Don't you miss our conferences?

ARIANNE. You're the one who dropped my course.

JULIAN. I thought it best, under the circumstances. You know, given what happened…between us.

ARIANNE. Nothing happened between us, Julian.

JULIAN. Nothing happened?

ARIANNE. What? What do you think happened between us?

JULIAN. I think we, you know…kissed.

ARIANNE. No. *We* did not kiss.

JULIAN. We didn't kiss?

ARIANNE. You tried to kiss me…

JULIAN. You're saying you didn't kiss me back?

ARIANNE. Look. Whatever did or did not happen, whatever you *thought* may have happened there when you startled me like that there in the library, didn't. Okay? And even if it did, it can't. It can't happen again. Not now. Not later. It's just not possible. Understood? Am I not being clear? Am I not getting through here? I mean my God Julian, in the library of all places. Do you know how many people could have seen us?

JULIAN. No one saw us.

ARIANNE. But they could have.

JULIAN. Well we're not in the library now, are we? This looks more like a bedroom.

(**ARIANNE**, *not amused, doesn't respond.*)

We can't still be friends?

ARIANNE. Friends? No. I don't think so.

JULIAN. Why?

ARIANNE. *(lowering her voice)* Because I obviously find you irresistible and I'm a married woman and I don't think it's a good idea for either one of us to be playing with fire like that.

JULIAN. Don't make fun of me. Please don't make fun of me.

ARIANNE. How old are you, anyway?

JULIAN. How old am I?

ARIANNE. Yeah. You never did say.

JULIAN. How old are you?

ARIANNE. Are you even twenty-five?

*(a beat as **JULIAN** refuses to answer)*

My God. You're not even twenty-five are you?

JULIAN. I'm in love with you.

ARIANNE. Julian. Please. My children are downstairs.

JULIAN. *(stage whisper)* I'm in love with you.

ARIANNE. *(stage whisper, too)* You are *not* in love with me.

JULIAN. But I am. I definitely am. I have all the symptoms. Trust me. I'm in love with you.

ARIANNE. What am I going to do with you?

JULIAN. Take me to Vermont.

ARIANNE. Stop.

JULIAN. Why won't you take me seriously?

ARIANNE. Because you're not being serious.

JULIAN. I thought you said your husband didn't want to move to Vermont.

ARIANNE. Who told you that?

JULIAN. Ah…you, I think.

ARIANNE. I can't believe I told you that. When did I tell you that?

JULIAN. Just before you kissed me, maybe.

*(when **ARIANNE** doesn't respond)*

I'm from Vermont.

ARIANNE. Shut up. You are not from Vermont? Since when?

JULIAN. Born and bred. You want to know how to make maple syrup? I'm your man.

ARIANNE. I can't believe I'm having this conversation.

JULIAN. *(continuing)* So your husband can stay here and I'll go back to Vermont with you instead. Easy. Problem solved.

ARIANNE. With me and my children?

JULIAN. Sure. I love kids.

ARIANNE. Probably because you still are one? Now, if you don't mind. I've really got to get back to...

JULIAN. To what? Get back to what? Two lives – three if you count your husband – hang in the balance. Now what could possibly be more important than that?

ARIANNE. Reality, maybe?

JULIAN. I'm in love with you. That's my reality.

ARIANNE. But I'm not in love with you. And since it really does take two to tango...

JULIAN. So you just like to kiss me, is that it?

ARIANNE. I didn't mean to kiss you. I'm sorry, if I, you know, was too stunned that you were kissing me... there in the *library* to withdraw more immediately. I'm a little slow, okay.

JULIAN. *(as he moves toward **ARIANNE**)* Sorry, but you can't fool me. I was there, remember? So tell me the truth. Just tell me the truth and I promise I'll leave you alone. Didn't you like kissing me just a little bit? Didn't you on some level, enjoy it one, little, tiny, bit? Can you look me in the eye and honestly tell me that you haven't at least thought about it. Wondered in some niggling little way where that kiss might have led...

*(**ARIANNE** hesitates just enough.)*

Ah ha! You have. You have thought about it. I knew it. I knew you had.

MELISSA. *(offstage or could actually enter here)* MOM. THERE'S SOMEONE HERE.

ARIANNE. WHO IS IT SWEETIE?

MELISSA. THE PIZZA MAN. ANOTHER ONE. THIS ONE HAS PIZZA.

ARIANNE. *(trying to exit)* Sorry. Looks like the Pizza man's here. The real one.

*(**JULIAN** grabs a hold of **ARIANNE** preventing her from leaving, suddenly much too intense.)*

JULIAN. What's the Pizza man have that I don't have?
ARIANNE. Pizza maybe?

*(***ARIANNE*** glares at* **JULIAN** *and down at her arm, suddenly fierce herself. He lets go of* **ARIANNE** *who moves out of the room. Reluctantly* **JULIAN** *follows.)*

(lights fade…)

Scene Four

(Setting: Mi Casa Su Casa, Mexican Restaurant.)

*(At rise: **MATT** and **MELORA** face the audience with a couple of Margaritas. They are watching their colleagues dance, talk, etc. At the moment, they have nothing to say to one another, but it feels comfortable. They both sip from their drinks at the same time.)*

MELORA. Everything okay?

*(**MATT** remains distracted.)*

Matt?

MATT. *(still distracted)* What?

MELORA. You hoo? Earth to Matt?

MATT. Sorry.

(a beat)

(trying to shift gears) Is it just me or are these margaritas like really strong?

MELORA. No, I'm feeling them too.

(They resume watching the others.)

(another awkward lull)

MATT. I wasn't informed there'd be dancing here.

MELORA. You don't like to dance?

MATT. Ah...no. Well, not in public at any rate. You?

MELORA. Sorry?

MATT. *(over the music)* DO YOU LIKE TO DANCE?

MELORA. Yes. I like to dance.

MATT. So if I asked you to dance right now, you might even say "yes?"

MELORA. I didn't say I'd dance with *you*.

(a beat)

Is Heather sleeping with Tad?

MATT. Technically speaking, I think they're still dancing. Actual sex probably comes later.

MELORA. I thought Tad was sleeping with Annie.

MATT. Last week. This week, he's sleeping with Heather.

MELORA. HEY HEATHER.

(She waves and smiles falsely at "Heather" offstage.)

(pause)

So is everyone pretty much sleeping with everyone around here?

MATT. Those are the only two I know about. Unless you know something...

MELORA. Don't look at me. I'm still pretty new around here.

MATT. So *you're* not sleeping with anyone?

MELORA. I'm pretty married, remember?

MATT. Hmmm...so, you've said.

MELORA. Meaning...?

MATT. Meaning oh, I don't know...just that you don't seem very married to me.

MELORA. How do you figure?

MATT. Well, you don't have any children for starters. Marriage without children is like...junior college.

MELORA. What?

MATT. A dress rehearsal. The minor leagues. And then there's that car you drive around in. What is it again?

MELORA. A Saab?

MATT. Right. A silver Saab convertible. Does that thing even have a back seat?

MELORA. Yes it has a back seat. It does.

MATT. Still. Not your typical married-person's car, you got to admit. Not to mention I've never even met your husband.

MELORA. You think I'm making him up?

MATT. *Are* you making him up?

MELORA. He drives a Porsche. My husband.

MATT. A Porsche? Really. Well, there you go. I mean a Porsche is like the least married car there is, edging out the Saab convertible. He really drives a Porsche?

MELORA. Okay. Go ahead. What mean thing do you want to say about my husband driving a Porsche?

MATT. I'm not saying it's the case with your husband, but I've just always thought people who drive a...*Porsche... ah* must be...oh I don't know, compensating for something? He's not little by any chance, is he?

MELORA. Little? He played right linebacker in college.

MATT. Really?

MELORA. Ron just likes fast cars.

MATT. How big is he? How big *are* right linebackers these days?

MELORA. Six four, 235? I haven't weighed him in a while.

MATT. Arianne's about five foot six, 120. She likes really slow cars. She drives a *Suba...ru.* A green Forester station wagon. Car seat in the back. It's a miracle if she ever gets it above fifty. I keep telling her it's got to be bad for the engine to drive so slowly all the time. The car probably thinks it's in a perpetual traffic jam. I mean what kind of life is that for an automobile?

(MATT starts to lead MELORA to another area of the bar.)

MELORA. Are we going somewhere?

MATT. Darts? I thought I'd challenge you to a game of darts.

MELORA. I should warn you that I'm pretty good at darts.

MATT. Yeah. Yeah.

(The two face the audience and start playing darts, tossing them toward the audience. Every so often they'll go retrieve them. It becomes clear by their facial expressions that MELORA is kicking his ass.)

So did I tell you I'm going to Vermont for the kids' Spring break?

(**MELORA** *shakes her head, "no."*)

I've told you Arianne kind of hates it here, haven't I? So we're off to scout Vermont out one more time. In search of the perfect town, the perfect house, the perfect life. Don't tell anyone, but we could be moving.

MELORA. Are you serious?

(**MATT** *nods.*)

Wow. That's kind of...big. Do you hate it here?

MATT. No. Not like Arianne does. I think it's a perfectly neutral place to live. Safe, easy, comfortable. Like Switzerland or something. And in fairness to Arianne she didn't know she'd hate it here when we moved. Although come to think of it, maybe she did. But then, you know, she knew I wanted the job – God knows why I did, but I did. Back then I did. And then the job thing sort of worked out – at first it kind of did – am I talking too much?

(**MELORA** *shakes her head, "no."*)

It kind of seems like I am. Maybe I'm getting drunk. It's a definite possibility.

(*They reach for their drinks. And then, completely synchronized, take long gulps.*)

So do you guys ever think about it?

MELORA. Moving? No. Why would we move?

MATT. Aren't you ever curious about other places? What you might be like in those other places?

MELORA. *(sarcastic)* Gee, Matt. No. Never. Of course I'm curious, but *this* is where I grew up. This is where my family, my friends are. Where my home is.

MATT. Well I guess we just haven't quite decided where that is. Home. *(He starts to chant it quietly and rhythmically to himself.)* Home...Home...Home...

MELORA. So you're seriously considering it?

MATT. *(continuing to chant)* Home...Home...

MELORA. This might actually happen?

MATT. It's just an idea.

MELORA. You do realize, of course, that the winters are like really, really long there? Like even longer than they are out here.

MATT. You've heard that too?

MELORA. I guess I just can't really picture you living in Vermont. Shoveling snow all the time in one of those red and black checked flannel jackets. Isn't that what they all wear up there?

MATT. Only the women.

(a beat)

So how long have you and…

MELORA. Ron?

MATT. *(continuing)* …been married, anyway?

MELORA. A couple of years.

MATT. Oh. Well, No wonder you don't seem that married. A couple of years. That's nothing.

MELORA. Well it hasn't felt like nothing.

MATT. Meaning…?

MELORA. Nothing really. Just hasn't felt like nothing.

MATT. Well, they do say it's the hardest. Whoever they are. The first couple of years of marriage, I mean.

(ignoring him)

Yes…? No…?

MELORA. Well, apparently I don't have much to compare it to. Not being all that married and all. You're really bad at darts by the way.

MATT. I'm having a particularly off night.

(a beat)

So you were saying about you and Ron?

MELORA. Oh nothing. Let's just say that this hasn't been the smoothest chapter of my life.

MATT. Oh yeah? And why's that?

MELORA. You don't want to hear about it.

MATT. Sure I do.

MELORA. No. You don't.

MATT. I really don't know how you could know that.

MELORA. Trust me. You don't.

MATT. I've actually got a pretty decent attention span for someone of my gender. I can even play darts really badly and listen. You want another?

MELORA. Sure.

(They stop playing darts, gulp their drinks. Then **MATT** *goes off to get more drinks.* **MELORA** *wanders back to the table.* **MATT** *returns quickly with fresh drinks in hand.)*

MATT. So. You were saying?

MELORA. About...?

MATT. About this not being the smoothest chapter of your life.

MELORA. So, I was *not* saying.

MATT. So, you were about to say.

MELORA. So, I was about to change the subject.

MATT. Jesus. Are you always this reluctant to talk about yourself?

MELORA. It's pretty personal.

MATT. Well, by all means, let's talk about the weather then. About what cars we drive. How great you are at darts and how terrible I am?

MELORA. And sad. It's a pretty, long, sad story.

MATT. Come on. Tell me your long, sad story.

MELORA. *(resigned, giving in at last)* Ron and I met in high school if you can believe it. First we were friends and then we did eventually end up sort of going out, but more like he needed someone to take to the prom and I needed to go with someone so why not go together since we were such good friends. That sort of thing. I wasn't much to look at back in high school by the way.

MATT. Yeah. Right.

MELORA. I've got the photos to prove it.

MATT. Is this the sad part of the story?

MELORA. So anyway, Ron finally just sort of broke up with me because…

MATT. …You weren't much to look at.

MELORA. Right. Well what he said was he felt quote "more like a brother to me than a boyfriend," unquote.

(a beat)

Ron actually had this younger brother, David, and he'd always been sort of around, back when Ron and I were…"friends." We would pretend to mind him hanging around, but…You look a little like him by the way. Anyway, I guess David and I sometimes flirted around a little with each other, not seriously…I mean he was like this, you know, annoying little brother most of the time. But there was probably something a little there that I just never really realized until I ran into him in college a couple of years later.

MATT. Ah. The plot thickens.

MELORA. I mean I barely recognized him. But there he suddenly was, only not so little brother-ish or so annoying anymore. He was actually sort of gorgeous is what he suddenly was.

MATT. So, he and I look alike?

MELORA. There's a slight resemblance.

MATT. So, you two got together.

MELORA. Yeah. And naturally it was all pretty awkward and everything, small world and all that, but just when everyone had kind of gotten used to the idea, Ron got sick. Cancer. He's fine now. But to make a long story short, Ron left school, moved back home and David and I ended up spending a lot of time taking care of Ron. And then David started doing a few stupid things…

MATT. Such as…?

MELORA. He started sleeping around…around and around.

MATT. Which is when Ron and you got back together.

MELORA. Right...So Ron gets better. Which was good. Which was very good. But David just continued to drift. He dropped out of school, traveled out West for a while and we pretty much never saw him until he finally shows up, completely unexpected, two days before the wedding. And after doing just about everything he possibly can to sabotage the whole thing he actually ends up being Ron's best man at the last second. But then immediately disappears again right after the wedding. Months go by. Actually, two years go by. And then finally, this past fall, David's on some back-country ski trip alone. And for some reason, no one can quite figure out, he decides to hike out into a blinding snowstorm alone dressed in like a raincoat or something.

MATT. So...did he...?

MELORA. Yeah. It took a while for them to find him. I mean we had pretty much figured out by then that he was dead. But we didn't *know*...we didn't know anything for sure until ten days later they found him lying out in the open in some snow bank, apparently with a big old grin on his face and a whole lot of drugs in his system.

MATT. Wow.

MELORA. Yeah. So...needless to say it's just been kind of a strange, complicated time for everyone. End of long, sad story. *(falsely cheerful as she raises her glass)* Is this why they call it "Happy Hour?"

(after a pause) What? What are you thinking?

MATT. Oh, I don't know. Just that we all have this, you know, stuff we're dealing with that we hardly ever get around to talking about...I've known you what, five, six months now, and we talk almost every day at the office.

MELORA. You wouldn't even talk to me for the first four months I worked here.

MATT. I wouldn't talk to you?

MELORA. Not until I cornered you there in the lunchroom and practically forced you to go running with me.

MATT. Still, I see more of you than I do my own family and not once does this come up?

MELORA. It just did.

MATT. Well, yeah. Sure. Now. After two pretty strong margaritas, me letting you win at darts, and a lot of coaxing.

MELORA. Like I said I barely knew you when it happened. I mean what was I supposed to do? Come into your office and say, "Hey, what's up? How was your weekend? What movies did you see? Oh and ah by the way, my husband's been really bummed out ever since his brother, the brother I slept with, froze to death."

(a pause)

So what are you dealing with? I mean what about you? What is it about you that I have no idea about?

MATT. Well, I was once a woman. There's that.

MELORA. Yeah. Well. That we had all pretty much surmised.

(She waits for him to answer seriously.)

MATT. Oh there's nothing. I'm as boring as a piece of furniture. Nothing ever happens to me anymore except I get to occasionally pull my back out emptying the dishwasher.

*(Their eyes catch. They stare at one another until **MATT** stretches, looks around, breaks the moment.)*

Wow. This place really fills up. What are all these people doing here, anyway?

MELORA. What do you *think* they're all doing here?

MATT. Really? All of them? So this is what's going on when I'm reading *Harry Potter* to my daughter? Amazing. Talk about your parallel universes.

MELORA. *(somewhat abruptly)* You want to just get out of here?

MATT. You want to go home?

MELORA. Maybe not home.

*(She leans into **MATT** and grabs **MATT**'s wrist and looks at his watch.)*

A little early for home. Unless you have to get home?

MATT. No. I'm fine. Out with all my best friends from work to celebrate the big FOUR-OH. We could get a bite to eat?

MELORA. We could. You okay to drive? I mean given your recent dart performance and all I'm not sure you should be attempting driving a car or operating any sort of machinery for that matter.

*(**MATT** does a quick check by closing his eye and barely does manage to finally touch his nose with his finger. He then touches **MELORA**'s nose. She smiles.)*

MATT. Apparently, I'm fine.

MELORA. Apparently you are.

*(They start to get up, gather their coats. As **MELORA** takes **MATT**'s hand and starts leading him out of the room, down the stairs, and possibly up the aisle of the theater she turns back to him.)*

MELORA. Matt, you can't move to Vermont. I mean it. Things would really suck around here if you moved to Vermont.

MATT. *(taken aback, touched, and then recovering)* Oh, who even knows? Who even knows what's going on with that?

(They're dancing only slightly as The Clash's Should I Stay, Or Should I Go? *starts to play loudly. Lights fade.)**

---

*See Music Use Note on page 3.

Scene Five

*(Setting: **MATT** and **ARIANNE**'s bedroom. Sometime later the same night, close to midnight.)*

*(At rise: The lights are off when **MATT** enters the bedroom. He tiptoes around, trying to undress and get into bed without waking up **ARIANNE**, who seems to be sleeping. But **MATT** can't help but make a bit of noise. He almost trips over **JULIAN**'s skateboard. After stubbing his toe on it.)*

MATT. Shit.

*(After he slips into bed, and lies on his side, **ARIANNE** suddenly pops up in bed and turns on bedside light. **MATT** tries not to act startled, but he clearly is.)*

You scared me. What are you doing still up?

ARIANNE. Gee, I don't know Matt. I guess I just couldn't sleep for some odd reason.

MATT. Well, at least I didn't wake you. *(referring to the skateboard)* What's that doing here, anyway?

ARIANNE. Where have you been? I've been trying to reach you for hours. Why didn't you answer your phone?

MATT. Fucking battery keeps dying. What is it? Are the kids all right?

ARIANNE. They're fine.

MATT. Then, what? What is it?

ARIANNE. *(distraught)* I don't really know where to start. Let's begin with your mother. It seems she thought she had a heart attack.

MATT. What?

ARIANNE. Indigestion as it turned out.

MATT. But she thought it was a heart attack?

ARIANNE. That's why I've been trying to get a hold of you. Well that was *one* of the reasons.

MATT. Because my mother thought she had a heart attack?

ARIANNE. Where the hell have you been?

MATT. But they're sure it's not one?

ARIANNE. Indigestion. Are you not hearing a word I'm saying? Why didn't you call? I just don't understand why you didn't at least call me. You're usually so good about calling.

MATT. But I did. I did call you.

ARIANNE. That was hours ago. So where have you been all this time?

MATT. We got some Chinese food.

ARIANNE. You were eating Chinese food for four hours?

MATT. There was a lot of food. I mean everyone always orders too much Chinese food. And, I guess I didn't get much lunch for some reason. And I don't know. It started to snow. It looked like it was snowing kind of hard there for a while, and no one else was leaving, and we just kind of got into this interesting discussion. For once. And to tell you the truth, with you being so exhausted all the time these days, falling into a coma every night at nine…And what does any of this matter when my mother's heart attack turned out to be indigestion?

ARIANNE. Because what if it had been a heart attack? I mean you said you'd be home by nine. You clearly said "nine." You could have been dead for all I knew.

MATT. Well, I'm not.

ARIANNE. Yeah, well *now* I know you're not.

MATT. Sorry to disappoint you.

ARIANNE. Don't be stupid.

MATT. I thought women didn't really get heart attacks.

ARIANNE. That's a complete myth. Hearts are part of our anatomy too, you know. They're not like…testicles or something.

MATT. Testicles? Now my mother thinks she has testicles?

ARIANNE. They did some tests. Ran an EKG or whatever it's called. She's home now. Resting from her indigestion.

MATT. Do I need to call her?

ARIANNE. Why? To find out she's still not having a heart attack?

MATT. She eats too fast. She's always eaten much too fast. The woman barely chews her food.

ARIANNE. Your father said it happened on the tennis court. The fake heart attack. Call her or don't call her, but either way, can you please come to bed soon and I can tell you the rest in the morning.

MATT. The rest? You mean there's more?

ARIANNE. Actually there sort of is.

MATT. Like what? My father thought he had a stroke on the way home from the hospital? My brother thinks he may have brain cancer?

ARIANNE. Well, the other big news, if you must know, is that you sort of missed your surprise birthday party.

(**MATT** *just stares at her, refusing to believe what he's just heard.*)

MATT. Tonight?

(**ARIANNE** *nods.*)

Here?

ARIANNE. This being your fortieth and all I kind of threw this big surprise birthday party for you and all your non-work friends. The only problem was that you weren't here. You didn't show up. So, there was no one to surprise as it were. I guess you could say that *we* were the ones who were surprised. Surprised by your *non*-attendance. Your unexpected absence. The uncomfortable fact that you simply were…well, not here.

MATT. Tell me you're lying. Tell me, please, that you're lying and I promise I'll forgive you for playing this really rather cruel joke on me.

ARIANNE. You know what I've decided? I've decided that a birthday party without a birthday boy is a little bit like a wedding without a groom. Not quite as embarrassing, but pretty darn close. Didn't we say nine o'clock?

And didn't you tell me tonight, on the phone, from the Mexican restaurant, that you'd be home by nine o'clock?

MATT. Are people still here? Are there people hidden away somewhere waiting to surprise me and this is payback for my being so late. *(calling out, wandering around to presumably call downstairs)* I'M SORRY EVERYONE. I'M SO SORRY FOR BEING SO LATE. YOU CAN ALL COME OUT NOW. OLLIE, OLLIE OXEN FREE.

ARIANNE. Jesus Matt...You're going to wake the kids. Pretty embarrassing, wouldn't you say? Not to know of your husband's whereabouts on the night you're throwing him a surprise party.

(a beat)

It almost evolved from this non-surprise birthday party into a search party, not that I've ever thrown one of those before. Although there was a bit of a problem with that, too. You see, we had no idea *where* to search. We did try calling just about every Mexican restaurant in town, just in case I somehow got the name wrong, but that obviously didn't really get us anywhere given you'd moved on to Chinese.

MATT. How many people are we talking about?

ARIANNE. Does it really matter?

MATT. I guess I'm just trying to picture it.

ARIANNE. Thirty? Thirty-five? Somewhere in there. Luckily no one from out of town. That would have been a real bummer.

MATT. And all day long I was feeling sorry for myself that no one seemed to be remembering that it was my birthday.

ARIANNE. Oh they remembered. We all remembered. It was you, it seems, who forgot. Who forgot to come home.

MATT. You should have said something. You should have told me. I'm not saying I'm blaming you, but come on. How can I be expected to show up on time for a party I don't even know about? I mean I never got the invitation! My invitation apparently got lost in the mail!

(**ARIANNE** *just looks at him.*)

I would have told you.

ARIANNE. Sorry for seeming so dense, but wouldn't that have ruined the surprise?

MATT. It would have been preferable to this. So what did everyone do?

ARIANNE. *Do?*

MATT. When I didn't show up.

ARIANNE. Do you mean did we have other party games to fall back on? Did we spontaneously start singing, "For he's a jolly good fellow, if only he were here?" And that's one of the tricky things about surprise parties. You never do know exactly when the person will show up. So it's hard to give up hope. I mean we were all pretty sure that you would, you know, *eventually* show up given that you do live here.

MATT. This is so awful. I mean this goes way beyond my usual birthday curse.

ARIANNE. You weren't even here.

MATT. Yes. I think you've made that pretty clear.

ARIANNE. It was almost like they were aware of some surprise party, missing person's etiquette or something. Cheerfully returning to their hiding places like good little children, although it was harder and harder to quiet them all down whenever we thought it might be you again. Of course everyone had started drinking by this point, but they all pretty much rolled with it. I was sort of amazed. Although there did get to be this point, oh I'd say after about an hour or so into it, when there was sort of a collective letdown. I mean it was pretty inevitable. It became hard after a while to simply pretend that you were just a little late. And then people did begin to feel a bit awkward as you can imagine, and eventually, apologetically, regretfully, began to sneak away. Not all at once mind you. There were the few diehards who did stay, of course but most of them left in these polite little groups around 10, 10:30. You could hardly blame them. And to tell you the truth, I felt relieved at that point. I just couldn't take all their tight, concerned smiles anymore and was pretty tired of acting like it was no big deal. My husband was missing. It happens all the time. You know, throw a surprise fortieth birthday party for your spouse and of *course* he doesn't show up. What do you expect? Most natural thing in the world. Some sort of version of Murphy's law. Happens to everyone at one time or another…

MATT. *(interrupting)* Arianne. Please. You got to stop. I think I might be sick.

ARIANNE. You were the one who wanted to *picture* it. You do have some nice friends, though, I will say that. Some real loyal guys who were more than willing to step up to the plate and offer half a dozen or more really good reasons why you were AWOL. Sam Carlyle even took me aside at one point in the kitchen to explain that forty just wasn't like other birthdays. And that perhaps you'd decided to do something a little crazy like drive to the airport to see if you might want to take a sudden trip somewhere. Trade in all your frequent flyer miles just so you could wake up in the Caribbean for a change of pace. Some version of How Matt Got His Groove Back. I guess he'd once had some friend of his who'd just taken off somewhere never to return. I think he actually *thought* he was being reassuring. Can you imagine?

MATT. Was Jack here?

ARIANNE. The last to leave. Jack even offered to drive me to the nearest precinct to see if, I don't know, there'd been anything that came up over the police radio, some sort of accident report, some sort of incident that might explain your whereabouts…or your non-whereabouts. It made me think, of all things, of that stupid television show where they try and track down missing people. That wooden actor, what's his name?

MATT. Robert Stack?

ARIANNE. That's the one. *(doing a fairly good Robert Stack imitation)* "On the night of February 17th, Matt Gordon went off to work, unaware that on that night, his wife would be throwing him a surprise fortieth birthday party." Jack might still be up if you want to call him. He gave me the impression that he doesn't sleep much.

MATT. Who?

ARIANNE. Jack. I would hate to be an insomniac. He seemed pretty concerned.

MATT. With comforting you, it sounds like.

ARIANNE. Mary was here too.

(a beat)

So, are you okay?

MATT. Me? Oh, yeah. Just great. Couldn't be better.

ARIANNE. You must have been having a pretty good time

MATT You're never going to forgive me for this, are you?

ARIANNE. Never? Never is a long time. But I will say this. I very much doubt I'll be throwing any surprise parties for you anytime soon. That I can pretty much guarantee.

(They are immobile. Then MATT finally looks around the room, not noticing that ARIANNE has sort of slumped in bed. At first the audience should also just think that she's simply closing her eyes exhausted, not realizing at first that she's fainted.)

MATT. *(suspiciously)* Hey. I didn't see any presents downstairs. Where are all the presents?

(After ARIANNE doesn't answer him, MATT actually gets to his feet and starts to search the room, opening

up drawers, looking under the bed, continuing, almost hopefully.)

If there were thirty-five people here tonight for a surprise party, there'd sure as hell be some presents to open, or did they boycott and take them all home?

(Finally **MATT** *opens a closet door and a stack of brightly wrapped birthday presents fall out onto the floor at his feet.)*

Found them.

*(***JULIAN*** then steps out of the closet, blinking, apparently just waking up.)*

Who the hell are you?

(when **JULIAN** *doesn't immediately answer, to* **ARIANNE***)*

Who the hell is he?

*(***ARIANNE*** then falls out of bed and onto the floor.* **MATT** *rushes to her, cradles her head in his lap.* **JULIAN** *is still too stunned to have moved.)*

Arianne? Arianne what's the matter? *(to* **JULIAN***)* Call 911.

JULIAN. What?

MATT. The phone. Call 911.

*(***JULIAN*** finally moves to the phone. Picks it up, holds it to his ear and listens for a dial tone.)*

JULIAN. *(still out of it, flustered)* Hey. Sorry, to bother you but what's the number for 911?

(blackout)

END OF ACT ONE.

ACT TWO
Scene One

(Setting: Earlier that same evening. Still the Friday night before **MATT***'s fortieth birthday. A snowy winter evening in February. We are now back at* **MELORA** *and* **MATT***'s workplace. The lunchroom. A large clock indicates for the audience that it's eight o'clock.)*

(At rise: **MELORA** *is offstage, presumably in the kitchen. There are cartons of Chinese food, quite a bit more than would seem necessary for two people spread out around the conference table unopened. As before, they are not drunk, but they've definitely had a few.* **MATT** *is standing on a chair for no apparent reason.)*

MATT. *(to* **MELORA** *offstage)* DO YOU THINK WE SHOULD HAVE MARKED OURSELVES IN? *(speaking to himself)* Am I in? Am I out? What am I doing here? I shouldn't be here. It's way past quittin' time.

*(***MELORA** *rolls her way on stage in a chair with her legs up. She coasts to a stop. Presumably she has heard some of* **MATT** *talking to himself, caught.)*

What?

MELORA. Am I...interrupting something?

MATT. No, I think we're pretty much done in here. So you really think this is okay?

MELORA. Okay?

MATT. Us being here. I mean being here at night. Eating Chinese.

MELORA. They wouldn't let us eat at the Chinese place.

MATT. I think they were remodeling. Take out only. *(a beat)* Are we still playing the game?

MELORA. The can't-touch-the-floor-one, you mean? Why, you don't like it?

(**MATT**, *still standing the chair might almost lose his balance.*)

MATT. Might just be ready for another game. Maybe the sit-around-the-table-and-stuff-your-face-with-Chinese-food-one.

(**MATT** *gets down from his chair and they move to the table.*)

So you really feel like this is okay?

MELORA. Like we might get in trouble or something?

MATT. Well we're not exactly here to work.

MELORA. Well I guess we *could* do some work if that would make you feel any better.

MATT. Well, let's not get carried away. Most of the time I don't even work here when I am here…to work. Are you sure no one else is still around?

MELORA. I very much doubt it. But even if they were, we're *allowed* to be here.

MATT. It's so quiet here at night.

MELORA. Hmmm. What time is it anyway?

MATT. *(checks his watch)* A little after eight. Why?

MELORA. Just wondering. Feels later than eight doesn't it?

MATT. So do you come here a lot at night?

(**MELORA** *laughs despite herself.*)

What?

MELORA. I'm sorry. It just sounds like some sort of line or something. "Do you come here often?"

MATT. Ah. Well. We both know that we come here pretty often, as in just about every damn day.

MELORA. I like it here at night. I tend to get a lot of work done. No distractions.

MATT. You're not like one of those sad workaholics who can't ever leave their work?

MELORA. Feel like a beer?

MATT. Alcohol levels dipping a little low?

MELORA. Could be. I think I saw some in the 'fridge.

*(**MATT** puts up his hand to signal that he'll get it. He exits to get the beer.)*

*(calling to **MATT** offstage)* IT'S STARTING TO SNOW.

MATT. *(off)* OH. THAT'S JUST GREAT.

MELORA. IT'S NOT THAT BAD. JUST FLURRYING A LITTLE.

MATT. *(off)* NO. THERE'S A NOTE HERE.

MELORA. AND IT SAYS…?

MATT. *(as he returns, reading it, duly)* "Don't even think about taking these."

(The note gets stuck to his hand. He tries to shake it free but it stays stuck to his hand like flypaper. Finally he shakes it off.)

MELORA. Oh. Well maybe we shouldn't then.

MATT. *(continuing to whine a bit)* But it's my birthday. And it's your birthday too. Yeah. Hey. Isn't that a song?

MELORA. The Beatles?

MATT. So you know about the Beatles?

MELORA. *(ignoring him)* Maybe they were talking about the milk, or an orange. How are you supposed to know if the note was meant to refer specifically to the beer?

MATT. Well, it was sort of taped to it.

MELORA. Ah.

MATT. Why is everyone so anal around here? I mean we'll replace it. Right?

MELORA. Right. Of course.

MATT. I mean maybe not today, maybe not tomorrow, or the next day, but eventually we will?

MELORA. We will.

MATT. I think I kind of hate everyone I work with.

MELORA. Really?

MATT. *(considers for a moment)* Yeah.

MELORA. Everyone? I mean everyone sort of means… everyone.

MATT. Not you, silly. If you wrote a note at all it would be something like, "Help yourself. Replace at your leisure."

(**MATT** *somewhat defiantly opens two beers anyway. He passes one to* **MELORA**, *who takes it with a smile. They look at each other as they take long swigs.*)

Fuck 'em.

(*They clink their beer bottles together and take another swig of beer. After a long awkward pause,* **MELORA** *shivers.*)

Are you cold?

MELORA. I'm okay. Rolling around on chairs sort of warmed me up a bit.

MATT. We could eat in my office if you like. Might be more comfortable. Or yours.

MELORA. Very funny. And actually I've been meaning to talk to you about that.

MATT. You want *my* office?

MELORA. *An* office. Actually just a door. A door that I could close. I don't even really require a window.

MATT. So you can write your secretive e-mails in private all day and then come in and do your real job at night?

MELORA. If I so choose.

MATT. A lot of work I'd end up getting done.

MELORA. I don't just write you, you know.

MATT. *(acting surprised)* Who else do you write to Melora?

MELORA. Well, they wouldn't be secretive if I told you, now, would they?

MATT. Is it Philip in accounting? He's kind of good looking in a boring Ken-doll sort of way. And then there's bad boy Tad. But that would be so unoriginal.

MELORA. You're going to have to plow me with a lot more alcohol than this to get those kind of secrets out of me.

(MATT watches her take a long gulp of beer.)

MATT. *(finally)* So what's Ron up to tonight?

MELORA. Ron? Who knows?

MATT. I'm always curious what other men like to do with their leisure time, not having any leisure time of my own to speak of. A bit of leisure envy, I suppose.

MELORA. Probably just hanging out with his loser friends. You know, the kind of guys who still live at home even though they're pushing thirty. Just now getting around to applying for jobs at Starbucks because their mothers have threatened to stop doing their laundry unless they fill out a job application every once in a while. And what they're really into is playing these weird computer games. What is it called? You know where they can simulate being airplane pilots of these huge commercial jets. Do you know the game I'm talking about?

MATT. *(uncertainly)* Terrorist?

MELORA. *(continuing)* And they have to land all these airplanes into these real – well, based on real…

MATT. Buildings?

MELORA. Airports all over the world. Paris or Rome, or even like, I don't know, some exotic airport in Fiji – if Fiji even has an airport, but something *like* Fiji – and they can try and land these airplanes in all kinds of adverse weather conditions. And they sort of compete, I guess.

MATT. Huh. But there are no passengers?

MELORA. Right.

MATT. No in-flight movie or snacks?

MELORA. Of course not.

MATT. No luggage. No overhead compartments. No frequent flyer mileage?

MELORA. I know. It's completely absurd. The airplane game is probably just a front and what they're really doing is sitting around checking out porn.

MATT. Sounds like a lot of fun to me. So what do they do? Call up on the phone and ask: "Can Ron come out and fly today?"

MELORA. More like: *(grunting)* "Ron there?"

(a beat)

So what about Arianne? What's the pretty Arianne up to?

MATT. Why do you keep calling her that?

MELORA. By her name?

*(**MATT** just gives her a look.)*

MATT. Well not flying any airplanes, real or imagined as far as I know. Most likely home with the kids, and cursing my name for not being there with her.

MELORA. I thought she was okay with you being out with all your friends.

MATT. Well she is. I mean at least in theory she is. We're all okay about our spouses going off and having some quality adult time of their own, away from wives and husbands and children. Until you're actually living through it in real time and the minutes are going by like hours and your husband is out doing.

MELORA. Yes…?

MATT. Non-children things like…darts. And the can't-touch-the-floor game. Eating Chinese. Drinking other people's beer.

MELORA. So how'd you guys meet, anyway?

MATT. We worked together.

MELORA. Ah. An office romance.

MATT. She was actually my boss. This was before she became a Professor. Involved with someone else at the time. Practically engaged to the fellow. But he, the other guy, was in Spain of all places for the year, doing some sort of hot shot international banking blah, blah, blah internship, and so things were already a bit shaky as it were for the long-distance lovebirds when Arianne found out that Charles had been sleeping with Penelope – I believe her name was. So. Anyway. When all those stars somehow aligned, I became sort of the go-to-guy as far as a little revenge sex goes.

MELORA. And you were only too happy to oblige?

MATT. It was thankless job, but someone had to do it.

MELORA. *(continuing)* And so let me guess. You were so hot in bed together that after that one time she never looked back? Was only too happy to be rid of Charles?

MATT. Not exactly.

(**MELORA** *just waits for him to explain.*)

Her plan, such as it was, actually worked though because back came Charles on the next flight he could get on, and thus ensued a month or more of intense groveling and apologizing and promising, to the point where I even think an actual date may have been set.

MELORA. For a wedding?

(**MATT** *nods.*)

Poor Penelope.

MATT. Who was also now pregnant.

MELORA. Wow. So what'd *you* do?

MATT. Waited it out, of course. Or tried to. I didn't have much choice.

MELORA. Sounds rough.

MATT. Well, it sort of was. But it eventually all got sorted out. It just took a while.

MELORA. A story with a happy ending. Who doesn't like one of those?

(**MATT** *stays quiet.*)

Still, adds a bit of pressure, though.

MATT. Pressure?

MELORA. Here you are, breaking up her relationship with a guy she was about to marry for crying out loud. I mean didn't you feel like, well, you better be really serious about this. You better know that this is *the one*, otherwise what are you doing breaking them up in the first place?

MATT. I think she's been in touch with him.

MELORA. What?

MATT. Charles. I think they've been e-mailing each other of late. You know, found each other on Facebook. Or rather he found her. They've "friended" one another, or whatever it's called. Some definite "friending" has been going on. You gotta love the English language. Who knew the word friend would ever become a verb.

MELORA. How do you know?

MATT. She told me.

MELORA. Oh. Well, if she told you. Nothing to worry about if she told you. Something to worry about if she didn't tell you. I mean lots of people do that. Find old friends on the internet.

MATT. Old *boyfriends*, you mean.

MELORA. Pretty harmless stuff.

MATT. Yeah. But old Charles, he's been through a divorce, and so…he might be trying to "more-than-friend" her. Maybe trying to second-wife her.

MELORA. Come on. You really think he's after her?

MATT. He's certainly sniffing around.

MELORA. Where's he live?

MATT. Back East.

MELORA. Oh. *(after a moment)* Where back East?

MATT. What?

MELORA. Where back East does he live?

MATT. New Hampshire. 'Live Free or Die.'

MELORA. But you said you might be moving to Vermont.

MATT. Have you not looked at a map recently? There's not a lot of border patrol between New Hampshire and Vermont last I checked.

MELORA. She wouldn't tell you she was in touch with an old boyfriend if she had plans to...

MATT. ...Fuck him?

MELORA. *Meet* up with him is what I was going to say.

MATT. Hook up. Isn't that what the kids are calling it?

MELORA. You're totally over-thinking this.

(MATT considers until MELORA abruptly jumps up, starts to exit)

MATT. *(calling after her)* Am I talking too much about myself again?

(MELORA exits without answering but returns quickly with a couple of candles and funky old bottles with wax drippings that have obviously been used before as candle holders.)

MELORA. *(cheerfully)* I just remembered we had these.

(MATT holds both of them upside down over his glass waiting for something to pour out of it.)

MATT. There's nothing in these. Beer pong?

MELORA. Candle holders?

MATT. Oh. I think I get it.

(MATT puts the candles into the candle holders. MELORA then throws a book of matches at him that he doesn't quite catch. They fall on the floor.)

MELORA. Bad catch.

MATT. Bad throw.

MELORA. Make yourself useful. Light some candles.

MATT. How festive.

MELORA. *(only a little suggestively)* And maybe later we'll blow them out and make a joint birthday wish.

MATT. Yeah. Right. As if we could ever agree on one.

(MELORA starts to take off her top shirt revealing a spaghetti-strapped tank top. She moves slowly, seductively toward MATT. Trying but failing to ignore her advances. Being ironic.)

And what would I wish for anyway, when I have so much already? When my life is so full?

(They kiss, tentatively at first.)

And what do we have happening here?

MELORA. *(through some more exploratory kisses)* Early birthday wish?

(As the two start to kiss more passionately the lights dim. And then silence. When the lights slowly come up, however, MELORA has returned to where she was before she moved to MATT. Her top shirt is back on again. MATT is staring off into space. And once they start repeating their lines again from earlier, the audience realizes that the above has been a vivid fantasy of MATT's that hasn't really happened.)

MELORA. *(only a little suggestively)* Maybe later we'll blow them out and make a joint birthday wish.

MATT. *(still dazed)* What?

MELORA. I said maybe later we'll blow them out and make a joint birthday wish.

(MATT retrieves the matches from the floor and lights the candles with a trembling hand one at a time throughout the following.)

MATT. As if we could ever agree on one. And what would I wish for anyway, when I have so much already? When my life is so full?

(MATT and MELORA stop and gaze intensely at one another in a suddenly serious moment as the lights dim…and The Beatles start to sing loudly "You Say It's Your Birthday…Well, it's My Birthday Too, yeah…")

(lights fade)

---

*See Music Use Note on page 3

Scene Two

(Setting: Even later that same night. An Emergency hospital room.)

*(At rise: **ARIANNE** is wearing a hospital gown. Almost immediately **MATT** enters, still dressed in the same clothes he has worn throughout the night, carrying a soda for him, and a bottled water for **ARIANNE** which he hands to her.)*

ARIANNE. Thanks.

*(They drink in silence. **MATT** is deep in thought.)*

MATT. *(finally)* So what was he doing hiding in our closet anyway?

ARIANNE. He said he fell asleep in there.

MATT. And you didn't know that he was in there?

ARIANNE. Of course not. He said he went up there to read or something, and then during one of our false alarms he went into the closet to hide I guess and then.

MATT. And then just fell asleep in there? Is the guy doing drugs?

ARIANNE. Maybe he hadn't slept in a couple of days. Maybe he's been pulling a few all-nighters of late.

MATT. So let's just say for now that I buy that. I'm still a tad confused about what this student of yours – this sleep-deprived, possibly drugged student of yours – was doing at my surprise birthday party in the first place.

ARIANNE. You mean the one that you missed Matt? The one that you never bothered showing up for?

MATT. Did he just show up?

ARIANNE. Yes. That's what I've been trying to tell you.

MATT. Came on his own. Even though he was never invited?

ARIANNE. Why would I invite a student of mine to *your* surprise birthday party?

MATT. I don't know. You tell me.

ARIANNE. I mean I guess I did sort of *eventually* invite him.

MATT. Eventually?

ARIANNE. He came by I think to maybe explain why he dropped my class, probably worried I'd give him a failing grade instead of just an incomplete. He didn't know that there was going to be a party, and then once he was already there, I just didn't have the heart to kick him out. He was actually quite helpful as far as assisting me with the set up. Can I have sip of your Coke?

MATT. It's not diet, you know.

ARIANNE. I just want a sip.

(**MATT** *then watches her gulp his Coke, and actually finish it.*)

There was hardly any left.

MATT. He's still here, you know.

ARIANNE. Who?

MATT. The guy. The student. Closet-man. Julian.

ARIANNE. You mean here at the hospital?

MATT. I just saw him out in the waiting room. With his skateboard. Says he wants to make sure you're okay.

(*We see* **JULIAN** *pace or perhaps even skateboard across the back of the stage, looking worried. He then turns and paces back offstage, though* **ARIANNE** *and* **MATT** *do not stop talking over his entrance and exit.*)

ARIANNE. Oh, for crying out loud. I fainted. Tell him I'm fine. Tell him he can go home. Go out there and tell him to *please* go on home.

MATT. I don't even know the guy. I found his wallet by the way.

ARIANNE. His wallet. Where?

MATT. In the closet.

ARIANNE. What were you doing in the closet?

MATT. Getting my coat. There was a condom in it.

ARIANNE. In your coat?

MATT. In his *wallet*. You don't find that a little strange?

ARIANNE. That you were looking through his wallet?

MATT. I don't even carry a condom around in *my* wallet.

ARIANNE. Why would you?

MATT. Does this guy like you or something?

ARIANNE. Like me?

MATT. Does he?

ARIANNE. I don't know.

MATT. Oh you do too know.

ARIANNE. Okay. Maybe. Maybe he does.

MATT. So that condom was maybe meant for you?

ARIANNE. What? No.

MATT. That condom had *your* name on it?

ARIANNE. Oh. Matt. Don't be gross.

MATT. Are you two having an affair?

ARIANNE. No.

MATT. Are you?

ARIANNE. No. I'm not having an affair.

MATT. Then what are you two having?

ARIANNE. Oh come on Matt. No one's ever had a crush on you at work before?

MATT. A crush?

ARIANNE. I don't know. Whatever you want to call it. I'm sure that they have but you're just too oblivious to even notice.

MATT. Did you encourage him?

ARIANNE. No. Matt. *No.*

MATT. It just seems like you're sort of enjoying this. Look at you, you're practically blushing.

ARIANNE. I am not. Oh Jesus. I mean, yes, maybe on some level I'll admit that I enjoyed the fact that someone other than my husband was taking a little notice of me. I mean I'm not going to apologize for that. I'm a middle-aged mother of two, who usually drives around in sweatpants because my jeans no longer fit. What do you expect from me? But that's all it was.

(**MATT** *doesn't know what to say.*)

ARIANNE. *(cont.)* Matt. That's all it was. I swear.

(*a pause*)

(**MATT** *gets up. Limps a bit to the window.*)

Are you limping?

MATT. I'm just a little stiff.

ARIANNE. Do you really need to run *every* day?

MATT. I don't run *every* day.

ARIANNE. I mean if you're worried about your weight…

MATT. …I'm not worried about my weight. Should I be worried about my weight?

ARIANNE. I just don't like to see you hobbling around, that's all. I mean you seem a little young to be hobbled.

(**MATT** *continues to stare out the window.* **ARIANNE** *picks up a magazine. She whips through it, turning the pages rapidly.*)

(*finally*) Why are you standing guard there at the window like that?

MATT. It's a nice night out. You can see the mountains.

ARIANNE. You can always see the mountains. Are they doing anything special tonight?

(*a pause*)

MATT. So are you really set on us going to Vermont for Spring Break?

ARIANNE. Just a bit of a non sequitur.

MATT. I just thought that after our last trip there that we were going to give this a bit of a rest. At least catch our breaths.

ARIANNE. No, that's maybe what *you* thought.

MATT. Everywhere you go, there you are.

ARIANNE. *Meaning?*

MATT. Just that you take your life with you.

ARIANNE. Something terribly wrong with our lives, Matt?

MATT. You're the one who wants to move.

ARIANNE. I want to *explore* moving there.

(*pause*)

MATT. Does this have anything to do with Charles?

ARIANNE. What?

(**MATT** *stays quiet.*)

Are you serious? You think I want to move to Vermont because of Charles? Oh, Matt. Is that really what you think?

MATT. I don't know. I don't know what I think anymore. I think that I'm tired that's what I think. I think I'm so tired of being stuck here that I don't even know what I think anymore. I mean what are we still waiting around for anyway?

ARIANNE. A couple of more "routine" blood tests to come back.

MATT. I can't believe you thought you might have been pregnant.

ARIANNE. I fainted last time I was pregnant. Twice, in fact.

(*a beat*)

MATT. What? Are you disappointed?

ARIANNE. I don't know.

MATT. Is that what you think we need right now? Another baby crawling around here?

ARIANNE. I don't know.

MATT. When was the last time we even had sex?

ARIANNE. What?

MATT. Sex. You and I? Just the two of us. Hard to have a baby when you're not having any sex. I mean when was the last time we even…

ARIANNE Maybe like…last night? After Melissa woke us up in the middle of the night? When I came back to bed?

(*a beat, as* **MATT** *starts to remember*)

MATT. That was you? You know I thought that was probably you. It looked a little like you.

(**ARIANNE** *can't help herself. She's amused. They share an uncertain smile.*)

You scared me. You know that? You scared the hell out of me tonight.

ARIANNE. That I might have been pregnant?

MATT. That you might have been dead. I'm sorry. I'm sorry that I missed my surprise birthday party.

ARIANNE. Wasn't very considerate of you.

MATT. No. It wasn't.

ARIANNE. And I'm sorry I didn't tell you ahead of time.

MATT. Well, just as long as you've learned your lesson.

(**ARIANNE** *stays quiet.* **MATT** *gets up to leave.*)

This is getting ridiculous. I'm going to go see if I can't spring us from this joint. At the very least tell closet man he can take himself and his condom back home if he hasn't already. That is if I don't punch him out first.

ARIANNE. Behave yourself, Matt. We've had enough drama for one night, don't you think?

(*as* **MATT** *reaches the door*)

Matt?...Is everything okay?

MATT. Okay?

ARIANNE. With us, I mean. We're okay, right?

(**MATT** *hesitates, not sure how to answer.*)

Well, that's not very reassuring.

MATT. No. I mean we're fine. We're good. It's just been a really, really long night, you know? I'm just trying to catch up here.

ARIANNE. Catch up? Catch up to what?

MATT. I don't know. My mother not having a heart attack? Missing my surprise birthday party maybe? Condom man suddenly bursting from out of the closet? You looking as if maybe you were the one having a heart attack?

ARIANNE. I'm being serious.

MATT. I don't know what you want me to say. Maybe it's just being forty. I'm always a little slow. Resistant to change.

ARIANNE. Well, the only thing we can rely on is that change does happen.

MATT. Who said that?

ARIANNE. Me, I think.

(MATT nods.)

(a pause)

MATT. You need anything?

(ARIANNE shakes her head. MATT nods. Gives her a vague smile and then exits. ARIANNE gets up, moves to the window, looks out at those same mountains. She turns back as if she expects MATT to maybe still be there. MATT, too, stops and looks as if he's deciding to maybe return to the room. ARIANNE realizes she's still alone – slow fade on both.)

Scene Three

(Setting: Earlier that same night. Back at **MATT** *and* **MELORA**'s *office. The conference room.)*

(At rise: There are now half-eaten Chinese food boxes strewn around the conference table as well as a few empty beer bottles. There is a messy, late-at-night feel to the place. It's snowing harder than it was before. **MELORA** *and* **MATT** *are sitting in chairs next to each other at the conference table.* **MELORA** *is staring at the candles burning down.* **MATT** *seems intent on peeling off the labels on all the empty beer bottles and making some sort of design with them on the table.* **MELORA** *cocks her head to the side to see what he's doing. She smiles, obviously approving of his odd artistic effort. She starts to join in.* **MATT** *admires what she's just done and continues.)*

MATT. Remember what it was like to be so young that you could spend hours doing some completely useless project like this and not feel like you were wasting time because you had so much time back then that you didn't even consider that you could waste it?

*(***MELORA*** smiles, watches him continue to "work" on his project)*

MELORA. *(finally)* So you guys are really talking about having another?

MATT. Oh it's one more idea. Like moving to Vermont. Probably a bad one. Hopefully never going to happen. We're just getting to that age where it's now or never. But I've talked to a few friends who already have three. And they say it's like a whole other deal. You go from man to man to zone defense.

MELORA. I can't imagine it.

MATT. What?

MELORA. Bringing up kids. Whenever I see anyone with children, it just doesn't seem that…what's the word I'm looking for? *Appealing,* I guess.

MATT. Yeah, well, other people's children rarely are. I'm not really sure why that is. Maybe to make sure potential parents give it more than just a passing thought.

MELORA. But yours are?

MATT. Are you saying mine aren't?

MELORA. I haven't even met your kids. I haven't even met your wife, remember? For all I know you're a guy who lives alone with a vivid imagination.

MATT. You want to know what makes parenting *interesting* to me, i.e. worth it in the end. I like it because it's not this instant gratification sort of thing. It's not like some Volvo commercial. Sunny days. Clean kids in clean cars in soccer cleats jumping out of the back with a golden retriever. Enough goals to go around that day so that everyone gets to score at least one and go home with a smile on their face. Most of the time no one scores a goal. And so someone's got their feelings hurt or are just simply feeling really low blood sugar and so they turn there in the back seat and for no reason at all hit the other one, hit them really hard in the arm or the neck, or sometimes even the stomach, the face. And one kid's suddenly crying, there may even be blood...

MELORA. ...This is the argument for why it's all worth it?

MATT. *(continuing)* Not always so *appealing*. But then it has these totally random and unexpected pleasures. Mostly when you least expect it. And I like that about it. The surprise. How things can change so much moment to moment. One minute everyone hates everyone and the next you're all laughing your heads off playing some stupid game of tag or something. How many chances you get to redeem yourself. Have you ever watched a kid sleep? Or read? Or just hear them laughing their heads off in the next room? You haven't a clue what I'm talking about, do you?

*(**MELORA** doesn't know what to say, stays quiet.)*

So what about your husband?

MELORA. Ron?

MATT. Doesn't Ron want children? Little Rons and Ronettes running around?

MELORA. Now there's a frightening thought. We've also got this slight other problem. I mean besides him being sort of absentee husband of late.

(**MATT** *waits for her to explain.*)

He's infertile.

MATT. I'm sorry. Did you say he's a turtle?

MELORA. *(laughing)* Turtle?

MATT. Slow to make up his mind or something? Sorry, I guess I didn't hear you.

MELORA. Well there's that, too. But no. I said he was *infertile.* All that chemo.

MATT. Ah.

MELORA. So he's shooting blanks. We did freeze some, though.

MATT. Wow. *(He nods.)*

(after an uncomfortable pause) Well, you've got plenty of time to decide. I mean, sperm keeps right? Especially when it's frozen.

MELORA. Yes. That's the general idea behind freezing it.

(a beat)

MATT. *(finally)* So where do you keep it?

MELORA. What?

MATT. You know…*(whispering conspiratorially now)*…the sperm. Ron's sperm.

MELORA. Not in our freezer with our wedding cake if that's what you're wondering.

MATT. No, I didn't think so. *(after a moment, unable to let it go)* Is it a secret? Is it buried out in your backyard somewhere and only you guys have a map in case of an emergency?

MELORA. If you must know, we actually keep it at this lab. It's like in some frozen vault or something.

MATT. The sperm cellar?

MELORA. More like a safe deposit box.

(**MATT** *looks at her, unable to stop himself from staring.*)

MELORA. *(smiling, a bit flustered herself)* What?

MATT. Nothing.

(**MELORA** *looks away, starts playing with the Chinese food but doesn't eat any more of it.*)

(a pause)

So?

MELORA. So.

MATT. What's going on with your bellybutton these days?

(**MELORA** *giggles at this.*)

I'm feeling a little bit out of the loop.

(**MELORA** *looks down and then lifts her shirt a bit, checking her bellybutton as if to make sure it's still there. She is wearing one of those thin gold chains around her stomach.*)

(taking a quick look himself) Everything looks to be in order. The way God intended it.

MELORA. My bellybutton?

MATT. Was there something else you wanted to show me?

(**MELORA**, *flustered, suddenly shy, lets her shirt fall back the way it was.*)

(after a pause) I like the chain.

MELORA. Thanks. I still haven't made up my mind about the, you know, whole piercing thing. I probably will end up chickening out.

MATT. It's a brave thing, to pierce one's self. I don't care what anyone else says.

(*Again* **MATT** *allows himself to stare at* **MELORA** *for a moment.*)

(feeling suddenly awkward) So Ron doesn't…he's not…

MELORA. Yessssss?

MATT. Worried? This wouldn't...

MELORA. Wouldn't what?

MATT. I don't know. Bother him, I guess.

MELORA. Us eating Chinese food together?

MATT. You don't feel the need to call him when you're out like this? Let him know what you're up to? When you'll be home?

MELORA. Ron's my husband, not my parent. And besides, Ron isn't really too interested in what I'm up to these days.

MATT. Somehow I doubt that.

(**MELORA** *doesn't say anything.*)

So what are you saying? That Ron doesn't really care who you spend your Friday nights with?

MELORA. *(proceeding carefully)* Are we now at the truth or dare portion of the evening?

MATT. Oh. So only you're allowed to ask the personal questions? Is that how this works?

MELORA. What was the question again?

MATT. Whether or not Ron ever gets jealous, or I don't know, whether you and Ron have a good marriage if you like?

MELORA. That's what you're asking?

MATT. Is it a hard question?

MELORA. It's just that it's a rather long and involved topic, don't you think? And I thought I sort of already did answer it back there at the bar?

MATT. Did you?

MELORA. I've got a question for you. What about women before...

MATT. *Before...?*

MELORA. You know.

MATT. Nooohhh...

MELORA. Other women? Before your wife.

MATT. *(pretending to be shocked)* Are you asking me how many women other than my wife I've slept with? Is that really what you're asking me? That's a fairly personal question Melora.

MELORA. And whether or not Ron and I have a good marriage or where we hide our personal reproductive stash *isn't* personal?

MATT. Only women I've slept with *before* I was married?

MELORA. You want to tell me about any *since* you've been married?

MATT. Now that's a *really* personal question. But...no. None.

MELORA. Wow. Really. That's impressive.

MATT. Impressive?

MELORA. Twelve years, right?

MATT. Twelve years.

MELORA. Never been tempted?

MATT. Tempted? Sure.

MELORA. What about your wife? Has she ever been tempted?

MATT. Well, I guess you'd have to ask her about that. But I think it's pretty natural, don't you?

MELORA. So were there a lot?

MATT. Before I was married, you mean? I don't know. What do you consider a lot?

MELORA. Let's say more than five, just for the sake of this conversation.

MATT. More than five? That's what you'd consider a lot? I mean I may not be any great shakes now, but in my youth I wasn't like totally decrepit and disfigured or anything. Hard as this might be to believe now, but there were actually a few women out there who didn't find me...well, repulsive.

MELORA. So I'm assuming that it is...*was*, more than five?

(MATT gives her a look.)

Okay. Fine. You were a total stud. More than five then?

MATT. Yes. More than five.

(**MELORA** *nods and then grows quiet, maybe a bit embarrassed.*)

Aren't you going to ask me if I slept with more than ten?

MELORA. The actual number isn't important.

MATT. Maybe not to you. So why did you want to know, anyway?

MELORA. *(shy)* I don't know. I guess I just sometimes wish I hadn't met Ron at such a young age. That's all. Happy now.

(**MATT** *nods, getting it*)

MATT. So you were probably a virgin?

(*after* **MELORA** *stays quiet*)

Both of you?

(**MELORA** *shyly nods.*)

Ah.

MELORA. Wow. I'm *really* going to regret this conversation tomorrow.

MATT. No. Why?

MELORA. *Why?*

MATT. I mean it is, I guess, a little unusual in this day and age, but also kind of sweet? Isn't it? Sweet?

(**MELORA** *doesn't say anything.*)

And then there was Ron's brother, right?

(**MELORA** *and* **MATT** *look at each other shyly and then away.* **MATT** *starts to pick at another beer label.* **MELORA** *watches him. After a long time they finally look at one another.*)

MELORA. What? What is it?

MATT. Nothing. I mean you've just got something…

MELORA. What?

MATT. On your lip. Something there on your lip.

MELORA. *(she starts to swipe at her face, licks her lips)* Do I want to know what it is?

MATT. It's just a piece of rice.

(He watches her for a moment.)

Other side. Got it.

*(**MATT** continues to look at **MELORA** intensely.)*

MELORA. Anything else I should know about?

*(**MATT** doesn't say anything, continues to stare at **MELORA** apparently lost in thought.)*

What are you doing?

MATT. I'm still checking. I want to be absolutely thorough.

*(**MATT** rolls his chair in even closer to **MELORA** so that they are now almost nose to nose. **MATT** continues to scan **MELORA**'s face intensely. Their bodies should be practically touching, overlapping.)*

MELORA. Stop. You're making me nervous.

MATT. I'm making you nervous?

*(**MELORA** smiles. Her hands go on **MATT**'s knees. Then **MATT** does start to slowly lean in, possibly to kiss her, but **MELORA** pushes away from him so her chair rolls away a few inches. She puts her head down, making it impossible for **MATT** to kiss her.)*

MATT. Oh God. I'm sorry. I shouldn't have done that. I'm so sorry.

MELORA. *(interrupting)* …No. It's fine. I mean it's nothing. Forget it.

MATT. No. I'm sorry. I don't know what I was thinking…

MELORA. …I think I may have wanted you to.

*(**MATT** just looks at her, a little stunned.)*

I did. I definitely wanted you to kiss me.

*(**MATT** just looks at her still totally confused.)*

(getting up, pacing) Oh god.

(She stops pacing, turns back to him. **MATT** *still waits.)*

MELORA. *(cont.)* Look. I wasn't expecting...expecting to meet someone like you, you know? Someone who I really, really like a lot.

MATT. *(interrupting)* ...Please you don't need to explain... you really don't need to say anything...

MELORA. *(continuing, ignoring him)* Think about, if you must know, almost all the time...When I'm here at work. And when I'm not here at work. When I'm driving in the car. At the supermarket. I look for you.

I do. Like hoping I'll somehow run into you. At first I thought it might just have something to do with your looks. You know, that you looked a little like David. And so it would probably pass. But then...well, it didn't. It didn't pass. It's gotten worse if anything. I mean, Matt, I hope you don't think this is something that I usually do, you know, regardless of how non-married I may seem to you. And so despite my relative inexperience, or perhaps because of it, if something *were* to happen...

MATT. What? If something were to happen...what?

MELORA. It's not something I could just forget about. Come in on Monday to work and act all nonchalant. Pretend it didn't happen the next day. Blame it on a few drinks. I'm not like Heather. Or Tad.

(a beat)

Not with you. Not with you.

(a beat)

Oh man.

MATT. What?

MELORA. *(pained, embarrassed)* Somehow that all sounded so much better inside my head than it did outside of it.

MATT. No. You're wrong. It sounded fine. It sounded pretty good outside of your head. It did. And I'm glad. Really

I am. I'm really glad that you said it. It was very... brave. It was.

(They look at each other tenderly for a long moment.)

I'm sorry. I like you so much too...I do.

(They share a moment, neither knowing what else to say.)

MELORA. *(finally)* But you're married. And you're moving to Vermont .

MATT. Oh, I don't know.

MELORA. No, you are. You're going to quit this job and move to Vermont and we'll probably never see each other again. You'll be around for a few more weeks, maybe a couple of months, it'll be a bit awkward between us, but we'll manage to mostly avoid one another and then eventually you'll take all your stuff out of your office and you'll leave. And whenever I walk by it, I'll think of you. Wonder what you're doing there in Vermont.

*(**MELORA** walks away to the window.)*

Well, of course that's what's going to happen...

MATT. You know if I wasn't married. If I wasn't so...damn married.

(After a long pause when neither one knows what to say to the other, **MELORA** *finally starts to clean up.)*

(noticing at last what she's doing) What are you doing? Don't do that.

MELORA. It's getting late.

(She continues to clean up.)

MATT. At least let me help.

MELORA. There's nothing more to do. We're all done. It's the least I can do given you having to play chauffeur all night.

(They stop, just look at each other.)

MATT. I am sorry.

MELORA. *(an attempt to be light)* Now you're not going to give me a ride home?

MATT. I feel bad about this.

MELORA. Bad? Why? Don't feel bad. You didn't do anything wrong. Come on, Matt. You're one of the good guys.

(a beat)

And I had fun. I had a lot of fun.

MATT. Oh yeah? And when was that?

MELORA. Tonight. With you. What? You didn't have fun? Well, that's a little insulting.

(They share a moment.)

(finally) So. You coming?

MATT. What? Yeah. I'll be right there. I'll meet you downstairs. I just need a moment.

MELORA. Sure.

*(**MELORA** starts to leave, but then turns at the door.)*

Hey, Matt? *(maybe about to say something else but deciding against it)* Happy birthday.

*(She smiles, then exits quickly. **MATT** stares after her for a long moment and then slowly starts to move around the room, clearing up whatever else **MELORA** hasn't picked up. He moves around the conference table and very deliberately puts the chairs back in their place. He then looks around the room one last time. At the door he takes one quick glance back and realizes that the candles are still lit. He moves quickly back into the room and then catches himself before blowing them out. He stands for a long moment, as if trying to think what to wish for. Finally, he leans over and with two short bursts of air blows them out. The stage goes dark.)*

End of Play.

OTHER TITLES AVAILABLE FROM SAMUEL FRENCH

MORNING, NOON AND NIGHT

Christopher Slade Newbound

Drama / 2m, 1f

Set on a muggy backyard patio in California, Morning, Noon and Night revolves around the disappointments and difficulties of the Smight family. Phil and Margaret, tired of each other and unprepared for aging, receive a welcome visit from their son John and his daughters. John informs them they are poised to move all the way to cold, rural Vermont, to Phil's dismay. Margaret, recovering from both alcoholism and depression, is considering leaving her domineering husband. Tensions build and old battles are rehashed in this quiet family drama, where ultimately, unfortunately, time must march on.

SAMUELFRENCH.COM

www.ingramcontent.com/pod-product-compliance
Lightning Source LLC
Chambersburg PA
CBHW071413290426
44108CB00014B/1809